Parkour
Defying Gravity

capstone
classroom

BTR Zone (Bridge to Reading) is published by Capstone Classroom,
1710 Roe Crest Drive, North Mankato, Minnesota 56003
www.capstoneclassroom.com

ISBN: 978-1-62521-114-9 (paperback)

Editorial Credits

Mandy Robbins, editor; Ashlee Suker, designer; Eric Gohl, media researcher

Photo Credits

Alamy: AF Archive, 28, 30; Corbis: Sean De Burca, 35; Dreamstime: Goruppa,
16, Olexa, 36; DVIC: U.S. Army/Sgt. Salli Curchin, 27, U.S. Army/Spc. Edward
Siguenza, 24–25, U.S. Army/Spc. Jared Forsyth, 22, U.S. Marine Corps/Cpl.
Tyler Main, 20; Newscom: El Nacional de Venezuela/Henry Delgado, 32, EPA/
Ali Ali, cover, 14–15, Getty Images/AFP/Giulio Napolitano, 10, MCT/Lyhne,
40–41, Mike Tittel Cultura, 4, ZUMA Press/Jim Weber, 12, ZUMA Press/
Manuele Mangiarotti, 9, ZUMA Press/Yannick Tylle, 38; Paris Match via
Getty Images: Maurice Jarnoux, 6; Shutterstock: 1000 Words, 33, Alexander
Smushkov, 19, Sunshine Pics, 43

Design Elements: Shutterstock

About the Cover

A group of young Palestinian men practice their parkour skills.

Printed in the United States of America in North Mankato, Minnesota.
032013   007223CGF13

TABLE OF —
CONTENTS

CHAPTER 1
A Rich History 5

CHAPTER 2
Core of Belief......................... 13

CHAPTER 3
Parkour in the Military.............. 21

CHAPTER 4
Popular Culture....................... 29

CHAPTER 5
Training and Techniques............. 37

Parkour Tips 42

Read More............................. 44

Internet Sites 44

Glossary of Text Features 45

Glossary.............................. 46

Index................................. 48

Bounding over high railings is a common move in parkour.

CHAPTER 1

A Rich History

He seems to be running for his life. He climbs fences, leaps over park benches, and slides down the handrails of staircases. He never appears to slow down. He never looks behind him. Soon he is joined by another runner. She too runs, leaps, and climbs over every **obstacle** in her path. But who is chasing them? No one is following them. They are practicing parkour (pahr-KOOR). They are running because they enjoy this extraordinary form of **athleticism**.

What is Parkour

Parkour is the art of dealing with obstacles, such as railings, fences, or even buildings, as part of running exercises. This full-body workout includes physical strength and mental quickness.

Parkour has been around for hundreds of years. Since the 1980s it has become recognized as an organized activity with specific skills and training. So where did this unique activity come from?

obstacle · something that gets in the way of or prevents someone from doing something

athleticism · the quality of being physically active and strong

The Grandfather of Parkour

The roots of this modern-day activity, or **discipline**, can be traced to Georges Hébert. Today he is known as the "grandfather of parkour." At the beginning of the 20th century, Hébert was a French naval officer. While serving overseas, Hébert watched the native people of Africa and the Caribbean island of Martinique. He was impressed with their physical fitness. Their fitness did not come from any organized training. It was the result of their natural way of living and dealing with their **environment**.

Georges Hébert practicing parkour in 1948

Inspired by these local people, Hébert imagined a new type of physical training. This training would consist of obstacle courses that required different types of movement. These movements included walking, running, climbing, and moving on all fours. They also included swimming, balancing, lifting, throwing, and the practice of **self-defense**.

Hébert's courses became known as *parcours du combattant*, which means "obstacle course." The obstacle courses he imagined were like those found in modern military training.

discipline · an area of study

environment · all the things that influence your life, such as the area where you live, your family, and the things that happen to you

self-defense · the act of protecting yourself against attacks

The Father of Parkour

Raymonde Belle was one of the soldiers who learned Hébert's style of military training. Belle was born to French parents in Vietnam. He became a French soldier and a firefighter.

During his military career, Belle became known for his physical strength, **agility**, and fitness. The method he used to improve his skills was influenced by Hébert. By doing many brave acts and rescues, Belle made a name for himself. But he also brought attention to the method he used to accomplish such **feats**.

Strong Body, Strong Spirit

Belle taught his son David much of his training. He did this through games they played. David learned a lot from his dad. And, like his dad, the younger Belle served in the French military and became a firefighter.

In 1984 David moved to the city of Lisses, France, which is right outside of Paris. The park in the center of Lisses is called Dame Du Lack. This park is known for its **architectural** climbing structures. It was there that David practiced the skills he had learned from his father.

In Lisses David found others who were interested in learning about his **maneuvers**. They formed a group called Yamakasi. The word *yamakasi* comes from the Lingala language of Africa and means "strong body," "strong spirit," or "strong person."

David Belle, 2006

This group's members were Yann Hnautra, Chau Belle, Laurent Piemontesi, and Sébastien Foucan. It also included Guylain N'Guba Boyeke, Charles Perriere, Malik Diouf, and Williams Belle. With David Belle as the leader, Yamakasi became well known. David and his group took their skills and turned them into a lifestyle known as parkour. People who do parkour are called **traceurs** (trah-SYOORS).

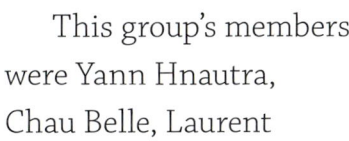

agility · the power to move quickly and easily; to be nimble

feat · an outstanding achievement

architectural · describing the style in which buildings are designed

maneuver · a planned and controlled movement

traceur · a participant in the activity of parkour

Foucan, 2005

Sébastien Foucan: Free Running

Sébastien Foucan was one of the founding members of Yamakasi. Foucan was born in Paris in 1974. He practiced and improved his skills in parkour. But Foucan added a new twist. He calls it free running. Foucan describes free running as finding your own way as a runner. Your own way does not have to be the same as anyone else's or one that has been defined previously. Free running is a very individual thing.

So, what is the difference between parkour and free running? Parkour uses the movements of going over, under, and around obstacles on a given course. It is going from one fixed point to another. Free running, on the other hand, is moving as an individual would through life. As one comes upon objects, they are quickly dealt with. Just as you would any obstacle in your life. Some say parkour is more defined, while free running is more open to new ideas. But both forms of movement take a great deal of practice, concentration, and agility.

A traceur bounds over an obstacle.

self-knowledge · knowing or understanding of oneself; one's character, abilities, and motives

martial arts · systems of fighting and self-defense, including judo, karate, archery, and fencing, that originated in Japan and Korea

competition · a contest between two or more people

philosophy · the study of truth, wisdom, the nature of reality, and knowledge

CHAPTER 2

Core of Belief

Parkour vs. Martial Arts

The basic idea behind parkour is that each person has certain abilities. These abilities help people handle everyday situations. Parkour teaches people how to use their abilities to tackle problems, big and small. It gives a person self-confidence and physical strength. More importantly, it gives a person **self-knowledge**.

Self-knowledge means knowing who you are inside. It is the understanding of your own nature and what you can do. When you have self-knowledge you know when to push yourself for greater gains.

But parkour is not a **martial art**. You do not train for self-defense or practice self-discipline as you would in the martial arts. Unlike the martial arts, parkour is not a **competition**. It is more of a **philosophy**, or basic idea or belief, about how life should be lived.

What Is the Value of Parkour?

To understand parkour, it is important to understand what it isn't. Parkour is not about entertaining. It is not about putting on a show. While there are flips, spins, and jumps, parkour is not a sport. It's not about how many flips you can do. It has more to do with how you feel after you have completed the flips. Parkour is a way of looking at the world around you. It is an attitude.

The feeling one gets after practicing parkour is what makes a traceur mentally stronger. There is a physical strength that comes from parkour. But this mental strength is an added bonus that many sports do not have.

Each traceur may approach an obstacle in a different way.

Self-Worth

Parkour is about **self-worth** and making oneself stronger physically and mentally. It is about pushing oneself to the limit and beyond.

An advanced traceur jumps between buildings.

Parkour

Running, jumping, vaulting, climbing
Muscles cramping, forehead dripping
Tired, sweaty, thirsty, but
Still ready for more,
Still have more energy in that core.

I am free, I have no worries
Wind blowing in my face
Sun beating down on my skin
Don't look down because you don't want to land there.
Always look up, it's where you should go.

No time to think of the jump
Keep moving, running
Heart beating, pounding its way out
I just realized I jumped off a one-story building and ran it
off as though nothing happened.
Precision is key.
—Anonymous

City and Nature

People who practice parkour do not see it as a sport. Because there is no competition, there is no need to outperform others. You compete only against yourself in order to improve.

Parkour is not just for city dwellers either. You do not need park benches, tall buildings, or cement obstacles to practice parkour. According to David Belle, obstacles can be found all around you. Wherever you look you can find places to practice parkour.

Climbing hillsides and jumping boulders can replace **urban** obstacles. In fact, practicing parkour outside of the city can increase **creativity**. Fallen logs, steep river banks, and tall trees can be your obstacles. This type of training also adds an element of peace to one's workout. Fresh air and wide-open skies can relieve stress.

urban · having to do with a city

creativity · the ability to think of new ideas

A traceur practices parkour on rocks at a beach.

U.S. Marines practice a training exercise on an obstacle course.

CHAPTER 3

Parkour in the Military

Hébert called his military training program "méthode naturelle," which is French for "natural method." He turned his program into a book. Hébert wanted his system of training to be available for others to use. His book, *Méthode Naturelle*, included many training activities to **master**. It also taught ways to keep from getting injured. Hébert's training method received high praise when it was published at the beginning of the 20th century.

Hébert's training was designed to take place on an obstacle course. Ideally the course would be in a natural setting. However, if no natural setting was possible, then the course should be made to resemble one.

Military Physical Education

Francisco Amoros (1767–1848) also deserves credit for developing the training principles of the French military and firefighters. His work focused more on making physical education into a real science, or area of study.

master · to become very good at a subject or skill   **21**

Does Parkour Have a Place in Today's Military?

Parkour has had great success as a training program for individual growth. But what do **backflips** and climbing have to do with the military? Some people see it as a way to use special skills in urban combat settings. Soldiers would be better able to pursue enemy **combatants**. However, many people who practice parkour have concerns about this idea.

A U.S. soldier hops over a cement obstacle during a military competition.

Parkour experts understand that the abilities to move and think quickly are important in combat. But they believe that some **elements** of parkour are not a good fit with military activities. One such element is clothing. Typically, traceurs wear clothing that is lightweight and comfortable. But soldiers wear lifesaving equipment, such as helmets and bulletproof vests. They also carry weapons. This equipment helps make them good soldiers. But it would **hamper** their abilities to turn and twist their bodies in parkour fashion. Soldiers also wear protective gloves on their hands. But traceurs say that feeling surfaces with their bare hands is essential to parkour.

backflip · a backward somersault in the air
combatant · a person fighting opposite oneself
element · one of the simple basic parts of something
hamper · to make it difficult for someone to do something

How Can Parkour Help Soldiers?

Because parkour encourages self-confidence, it can be an important tool in training soldiers. In combat soldiers must have confidence in their abilities and actions. Combat is not the time for soldiers to second-guess their training.

Parkour also helps improve the mind. Being able to think quickly in constantly changing surroundings is one of the benefits of practicing parkour. Parkour also helps soldiers improve their reflexes.

U.S. Army soldiers train on an obstacle course.

People who enter the military with experience in parkour tend to do better in **basic training** tests. This often results in advanced placement for them. It also gives them greater confidence to tackle whatever future challenges come their way.

basic training · the first training period for people who join the military; basic training is sometimes called boot camp

Future Military Training

Can parkour training improve results on the battlefield? It is uncertain what influence parkour will have on the armies of the future. But many believe that as warfare changes, training must change as well.

However, some things never change. A successful army is well trained. A successful soldier must be strong and **self-assured**. Therefore, it would seem that parkour can be a very useful part of military training.

Obstacle Course

Obstacle courses designed for military training are meant to test strength, agility, and **endurance**. They usually involve these skills, all of which are important to parkour and free running:

- jumping
- dodging
- climbing
- **traversing**
- crawling
- **vaulting**
- balancing

An army sergeant competes in a National Guard obstacle course.

self-assured · being confident in one's own abilities

endurance · the ability to keep doing an activity for long periods of time

traverse · to travel across or over

vault · to leap over something using your hands or other support

David Belle demonstrates his parkour skills in a scene from the 2004 French film.

CHAPTER 4

Popular Culture

Parkour Is Everywhere!

People commonly practice parkour in big cities. Parkour clubs, organizations, online chat rooms, and video games are becoming more popular. You will often find traceurs in the same places skateboarders like to practice. Both groups use concrete steps, tunnels, handrails, and ramps to do their tricks.

David Belle has brought parkour to a larger audience through his work in movies. These movies show Belle performing extraordinary parkour moves. He is seen leaping from buildings, gliding down drain pipes, and jumping over apartment railings with great ease. In such scenes he is typically fleeing from people who want to kill him. But he doesn't stop and fight. He is not a fighter. He is a master traceur, and these movie scenes are an exciting way to show how parkour can be used.

Sébastien Foucan in the
2006 James Bond movie,
Casino Royale

Lights, Camera, Action!

Have you seen parkour in movies?
Have you seen it on TV? Parkour and free
running were first seen on screen in small
homemade movies starring some of the
original members of Yamakasi. As parkour
and free running became more popular,
some Yamakasi members were able to get
bigger parts in professional movies. David
Belle and Sébastien Foucan have become
action stars.

Big Hollywood films have also caught parkour fever. Parkour was featured in the film *Live Free or Die Hard* (2007), which stars Bruce Willis. *Sherlock Holmes: A Game of Shadows* (2011) and the blockbuster movie *Hunger Games* (2012) also featured parkour. Free running was featured in the movie *Casino Royale* (2006), with Sébastien Foucan making the moves. Filmgoers loved the action and suspense free running added to the film.

A traceur gets big air while practicing parkour.

Life or Video Game?

One fun aspect of playing video games is that you never know what might be coming up next. You always have to be ready for the unexpected. Getting from one place to another without getting hurt describes both gaming and parkour. In games like *Super Mario* and *Sonic the Hedgehog* you can see parkour moves. Have you ever wanted to do some of the things that Mario and his brothers do in the video games? Have you ever wanted to leap high and land without hurting yourself? How about jumping a stream without losing a step? Leaping fences, sliding down poles, and jumping open spaces are not only for video-game characters!

Playing video games successfully requires the player to react to challenges quickly. Therefore, it is not surprising to see many video games that feature the qualities of parkour. This brings up interesting questions. Do video game characters imitate real life? Or is real life influenced by video games?

Mario and Luigi are off and running!

Parkour for Women

Parkour is not just for men. Many women enjoy the rigorous discipline of parkour. They develop strength and endurance while pushing their bodies to new limits. Safety and proper conditioning are even more important for female traceurs than for males, though. Women are more prone to knee injuries.

Women play a big role in the parkour community. If you've seen or read *The Hunger Games*, you will remember how Katniss Everdeen needed parkour skills to survive.

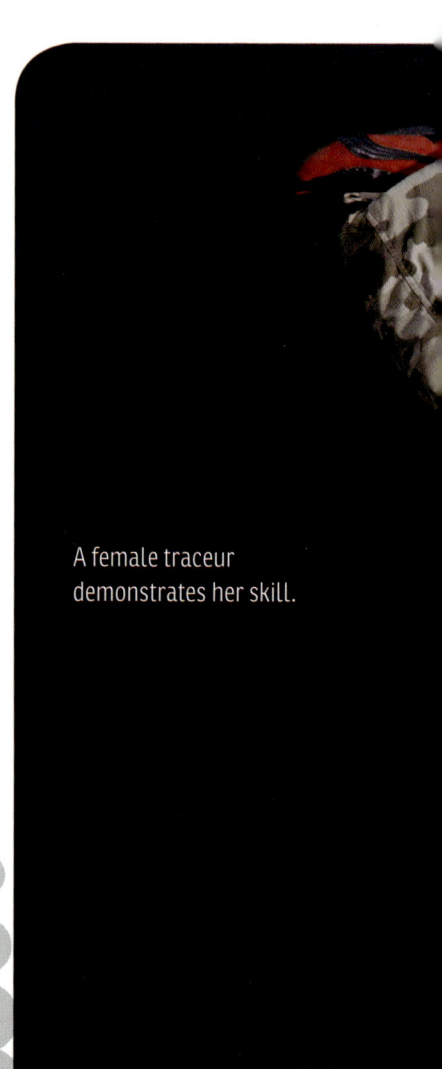

A female traceur demonstrates her skill.

It is important to remember that parkour is not about competition. The only person a traceur has to beat is herself. Everyone can be better than they used to be.

A traceur practices landing and rolling off of a building.

CHAPTER 5

Training and Techniques

Parkour athletes undergo training before attemptiong this sport. First, they need to increase their endurance. They begin by doing basic exercises including push-ups, sit-ups, pull-ups, and squats. These exercises help them establish a firm foundation, or base. Most experts agree that parkour athletes should be able to do 25 push-ups, five pull-ups, and 50 full squats before beginning the next level of training.

Now for Some Moves

Parkour athletes also practice landings and rolling. These are important skills to help keep them safe. Along the way, they keep up with basic training and strength endurance.

Next, athletes add vaulting, jumping, and climbing to their training. These moves are more difficult. Traceurs start low to the ground and work their way up. At this point, they start to develop their own style of parkour. And they always try to practice their skills safely.

Practice Makes Perfect

To do well in parkour, athletes must practice at least two to three times a week. When not practicing their parkour moves, they keep up their endurance training. It takes time to improve, but progress does come. Traceurs take their training very seriously. Practice makes perfect.

A group of traceurs warms up before practicing parkour.

Listen to Your Body

Traceurs always warm up before starting parkour. Stretched muscles perform better. Traceurs take a break if their muscles become sore. Sore muscles need rest before they can function well again. Sometimes a traceur's hands hurt or sting. But this may be a good sign. It means they are giving them a good workout. Their hands will heal and get stronger with time.

Traceurs listen to their bodies, especially if they have any breathing limitations such as asthma. Traceurs don't do parkour if they are wheezing. They always have an inhaler (asthma medication) in case breathing problems arise during training.

What Do Traceurs Say About Parkour?

Traceurs have a lot to say about parkour. They want to show others how to practice parkour safely. They also want parkour to fulfill the lives of others as it has fulfilled theirs.

Shaun Andrews, a traceur, believes that fear can be a traceur's biggest enemy. His message: Overcome your fears; don't let them stand in your way of success. By overcoming your fears you will gain confidence in yourself.

Basic Parkour Maneuvers

Landing

Underbar

Cat Leap

Wall Run

PARKOUR

Traceur Chris Hayes-Kossman thinks that by improving and building on past successes, you can begin to do more complex moves. The more complex the moves, the better you will feel about yourself.

Finally, David Belle reminds traceurs that parkour is about finding ways out of emergency situations. If someone were chasing you, which way would you move? What movements would you use? How would you overcome the situation? This is an important part of parkour.

Diving Kong **Tic Tac** **Lache**

Depend upon rapid redistribution of body weight

Absorption and redistribution of energy are important factors

High speed, good jumping, and landing techniques are important

Train body and mind to react to obstacles appropriately with a technique that works

Parkour Tips

To enjoy parkour you must learn to

- respect yourself
- respect others
- respect your environment

Ten Safety Tips

1. Always have someone with you when you practice parkour.

2. Always warm up and stretch before you begin parkour.

3. Wear shoes that protect your feet. Shoes should be light so they won't slow you down.

4. Wear clothing that allows you to move freely. Jeans are not good parkour gear.

5. Start slowly.

6. Begin training on a floor or flat surface. Once you have mastered a skill you can move to a more difficult location.

7. Don't go beyond your limits and training.

8. Listen to your body! If something really hurts or if you are dizzy—stop!

9. Find your own way of performing jumps, leaps, and climbs. Don't depend on the methods of other people. You know what your body is capable of better than anyone.

10. Research all you can, and learn from others who do parkour.

Training with a friend is safer and can be more fun.

Read More

Cohn, Jessica. *Free Running.* Incredibly Insane Sports. New York: Gareth Stevens Pub., 2013.

Edwardes, Dan. *Parkour.* Crabtree Contact. New York: Crabtree Pub. Co., 2009.

Mason, Paul, and Sarah Eason. *Free Running.* On the Radar: Sports. Minneapolis: Lerner Publications, 2012.

Teller, Jackson. *Free Running.* Adrenaline Rush. Mankato, Minn.: Smart Apple Media, 2013.

Internet Sites

FactHound offers a safe, fun way to find Internet sites related to this book. All of the sites on FactHound have been researched by our staff.

Here's all you do:
Visit *www.facthound.com*
Type in this code: 9781625211149

Check out projects, games and lots more at
www.capstonekids.com

Glossary
of Text Features

Text Feature	How to Use it
Caption: A word or group of words shown with a picture or illustration	Read a caption to understand information that may not be in the text.
Diagram: A drawing that shows or explains something	Examine a diagram to understand steps in a process, how something is made, or the parts of something.
Glossary: List of key terms with their meanings	Look up key terms in the glossary to find their meanings and to get a better understanding of the topic of the text.
Index: Alphabetical list of key terms, names, and topics in a text with their page numbers	Use the index to find pages that contain information you are looking for.
Map: A drawing that represents a place, such as a country or city	Use a map to understand relative locations and determine where events took place.
Photograph or Illustration: Visuals that are created by cameras or drawn	Examine photographs and illustrations to better understand ideas in the text that might be unclear.
Subhead: Word or group of words that divides the text into sections and tells the main idea of a section	Use subheads to locate information in the text and understand how a text is organized.
Table: Represents data in a small space	Examine a table to understand data or to compare information in the text.
Table of Contents: List of the major parts of the book and their page numbers	Use a table of contents to locate general information in the text and see how the topics are organized.
Text Box: A box in the text that provides extra information about a topic	Read a text box to understand interesting or important information.
Text Style: Bold, color, or italic words in the text	Pay attention to bold, italic, and color to figure out which words in the text are important words.
Timeline: Shows events in the order in which they occurred	Use a timeline to understand the order in which events occurred or how one event led to another.

Glossary

agility (uh-GI-luh-tee) • the power to move quickly and easily; to be nimble

architectural (ar-ki-TEK-chur-uhl) • describing the style in which buildings are designed

athleticism (ath-LET-uh-siz-uhm) • the quality of being physically active and strong

backflip (BAK-flip) • a backward somersault in the air

basic training (BAYS-ic TRAIN-ing) • the first training period for people who join the military; basic training is sometimes called boot camp

combatant (com-BAT-uhnt) • a person fighting opposite oneself

competition (kahm-puh-TI-shuhn) • a contest between two or more people

creativity (kree-ay-TI-vuh-tee) • the ability to think of new ideas

discipline (DISS-uh-plin) • an area of study

element (EL-uh-muhnt) • one of the simple basic parts of something

endurance (en-DUR-enss) • the ability to keep doing an activity for long periods of time

environment (en-VYE-ruhn-muhnt) • all the things that influence your life, such as the area where you live, your family, and the things that happen to you

feat (FEET) • an outstanding achievement

fitness (FIT-nuhs)—a person's health and strength

hamper (HAM-pur) • to make it difficult for someone to do something

maneuvers (muh-NOO-ver) • a planned and controlled movement

martial arts (MAR-shuhl ARTS) · systems of fighting and self-defense, including judo, karate, archery, and fencing, that originated in Japan and Korea

master (MASS-tuhr) · to become very good at a subject or skill

obstacle (OB-stuh-kuhl) · something that gets in the way or prevents someone from doing something

philosophy (fuh-LOSS-uh-fee) · the study of truth, wisdom, the nature of reality, and knowledge

self-assured (SELF uh-SHURD) · being confident in one's own abilities

self-defense (SELF-di-FENSS) · the act of protecting yourself against attacks

self-knowledge (SELF-NOL-ij) · knowing or understanding of oneself; one's character, abilities, and motives

self-worth (SELF-WURTH) · feelings of pride and respect for yourself

traceur (trah-SUR) · a participant in the activity of parkour

traverse (truh-VURS) · to travel across or over

urban (UR-buhn) · having to do with a city

vault (VAWLT) · to leap over something using your hands or other support

Index

Belle, David, 8–9, 18, 29, 30, 41
Belle, Raymonde, 8

Casino Royale, 31
clothing, 23, 42

Dame Du Lack, 8

Foucan, Sébastien, 9, 10, 30, 31
free running, 10–11, 30, 31

Hébert, Georges, 6–7, 8, 21
Hunger Games, 31, 34

Lisses, France, 8–9
Live Free or Die Hard, 31

Martinique, 6
Méthode Naturelle, 21
military, 8, 21–26

philosophy, 13–16, 42

safety, 37, 40

traceurs, 9, 15, 23, 29, 34, 35, 37, 38, 39, 40, 41
training, 5, 6, 7, 8, 18, 21, 22, 24, 26, 37–42

video games, 29, 32–33

Yamakasi, 9, 10, 30

Index

Allies, 30, 31, 36, 40, 41
Apollo 11, 42, 44
Area 51, 15
Armstrong, Neil, 42
atomic bombs, 27, 29, 33, 36, 37, 40
Axis, 30, 31, 32

B-2 stealth bombers 6, 7, 9
biometrics 23, 24

Central Intelligence Agency (CIA), 51
Cold War, 40, 41

drones, 56, 57, 58, 59

Einstein, Albert, 32
electronic footprints, 16, 17, 18

Fermi, Enrico, 32
fission, 28, 29, 30, 32
Fuchs, Klaus, 36, 40

Gagarin, Yuri, 38
Gemini missions, 44
global positioning system (GPS),12, 13, 18
Groves, Leslie, 32, 33

Kennedy, John F., 42

Manhattan Project, the, 27, 32, 33, 34, 36
Mercury missions, 44, 47, 49
missiles, 10, 14, 40, 42

NASA, 42, 44, 47
National Security Agency (NSA), 18
New Mexico, 26, 27, 33, 34

Oak Ridge, Tennessee, 34, 35
Oppenheimer, Robert, 32, 33

Powers, Gary, 50, 51

radar, 8, 9
Ride, Sally, 48
robots, 5, 56, 57

satellites, 4, 5, 12, 39, 44, 48, 52, 53, 55, 57
Shepard, Alan, 38
smart bombs, 10–13
Soviet Union, 30, 31, 36, 38, 39, 40, 48, 51
space capsules, 45, 47, 48, 49
space race, 39, 41, 45, 46
Sputnik I, 39
Sputnik II, 46

Tereshkova, Valentina, 48

U-2 spy planes, 50, 51
uranium, 29, 34

Vostok missions, 49

World War II, 30–31, 37, 40, 41

exhaust (eg-ZAWST) • the waste gases produced by an engine

fission (FI-shuhn) • the splitting apart of the nucleus of an atom to create large amounts of energy

friction (FRIK-shuhn) • a force created when two objects rub together; friction slows down objects

global positioning system (GLOH-buhl puh-ZI-shuh-ning SISS-tuhm) • an electronic tool used to find the location of an object; this system is often called GPS

gravity (GRAV-uh-tee) • a force that pulls objects with mass together; gravity pulls objects down toward the center of Earth

infrared (IN-fruh-red) • light that produces heat; humans cannot see infrared light

iris (AHY-ris) • the round colored part of your eye

laser (LAY-zur) • a device that uses radiation to create a powerful beam of energy

microchip (MYE-kroh-chip) • a device in a computer that sends and stores information

nucleus (NOO-klee-uhss) • the center of an atom; a nucleus is made up of neutrons and protons

offensive weapons (uh-FEN-siv WEP-uhns) • military weapons used to attack an enemy

orbit (OR-bit) • the path an object follows as it goes around the Sun or a planet

Periodic table (PIHR-ee-od-ik TAY-buhl) • chart of the chemical elements arranged according to their atomic numbers

physicist (FIZ-uh-sist) • a scientist who studies matter and energy

pupil (PYOO-puhl) • the round, dark center of your eye that lets in light

radar (RAY-dar) • a device that uses radio waves to track the location of objects

radiation (ray-dee-AY-shuhn) • rays of energy given off by certain elements

satellite (SAT-uh-lite) • a spacecraft that circles Earth; satellites gather and send information

vein (VAYN) • a blood vessel that carries blood back to the heart

X-ray (EKS-ray) • a picture taken of the inside of the body